The Best 50
MUFFIN RECIPES

Karen L. Pepkin

Bristol Publishing Enterprises
Hayward, California

Printed in the United States of America.
ISBN: 1-55867-320-2

Cover design: Frank J. Paredes
Cover photography: John A. Benson
Food Styling: Randy Mon
Illustrations: Nora Wylde

WHAT IS A MUFFIN?

According to Random House Webster's Unabridged Dictionary, a muffin is "an individual cup-shaped quick bread made with wheat flour, corn meal or the like, and baked in a pan," but this definition only scratches the surface. In this book, the range of muffins has been expanded from the traditional blueberry, corn or banana to cherry vanilla, feta herb, orange pineapple and many more!

These fifty recipes include variations; however, your own creativity can expand that number even more. Feel free to experiment with different flours, fruits and add-ins such as dried fruits, nuts, meats and cheeses. Or vary the amount of add-ins. The possibilities are endless.

The book is divided into two parts, "Sweet Muffins" and "Meals-in-a-Muffin." A Sweet Muffin is like a dessert. It tends to be very moist and cake like, making an excellent breakfast or snack. A "Meal-in-a-Muffin" is exactly that. Grab it for a quick breakfast or lunch on the go. Add a salad or soup for a more balanced meal. It's especially good when warm so serve it slightly heated if you can. It helps to release the flavor.

To be sensitive to the needs of those following a more restrictive diet or those who are health conscious, I have designated those recipes that are low fat/high fiber with a ♥ symbol, and included specific substitutes to reduce fat and calories. Using egg substitute, 2% reduced fat milk and eliminating nuts are always an option.

Lastly, ENJOY ... ENJOY ... ENJOY!!!

DEDICATION

This book is dedicated to my mother, Esther S. Pepkin, and my grandmother, Rose Kirschenbaum Scherick, who were my first culinary teachers.

ACKNOWLEDGMENTS

I want to thank Cris Mueller, Kathy Duval and Glen Duval, who functioned as my test kitchen, giving me invaluable feedback. I also want to thank Wendell C. Taylor, without whose constant prodding, this book would never have been published.

MUFFIN TIPS

1. Remember, ovens and climates vary. Try baking a recipe using the minimum amount of time, and if necessary, increase in increments of three minutes.

2. Muffins are very adaptable. Use your creativity to come up with variations, but begin by following the recipes as written.

3. Avoid over-mixing muffin batters; mix batter just until ingredients are blended.

4. Muffins can be stored in the refrigerator or freezer, but not indefinitely. They are best eaten soon after they are baked.

5. Muffins continue to bake after you take them out of the oven. Keep this in mind to avoid overcooking.

6. Always let muffins cool to room temperature before removing them from the muffin pan.

7. Margarine and eggs are best used at room temperature.

8. Use a toothpick to test whether muffin is done. Pierce muffin in the thickest part. If it comes out with batter clinging, it needs more time. Muffins are done as soon as a toothpick comes out clean.

9. Some muffins containing fruits or chips can stick, despite using a Teflon pan or cooking spray. To remove them after they have cooled, either go around each cup with a knife, or gently twist each muffin before removing it.

10. The muffin pans used in this cookbook are all standard size (3 inches across and 1 inch deep). The final product is not a large, commercial-size product but a small gem.

11. Muffins can be reheated by placing them in a microwave oven for 15 seconds.

VERSATILE, INFINITE-POSSIBILITY, BRAN MUFFINS ♥

This low-fat, high-fiber recipe is very heart-healthy. There are, as the title suggests, lots of variations: you are only limited by your creativity. The basic recipe is not very sweet, so add extra ingredients or serve it with jam or jelly if you prefer a sweeter taste. It has a hearty texture and is perfect for breakfast or a snack.

nonstick cooking spray
1 egg
2 tbs. vegetable oil
4 tbs. honey
1 cup low-fat buttermilk
1 cup bran

1¼ cup whole-wheat flour
1 tsp. baking powder
1 tsp. baking soda
¼ tsp. salt
½ cup chopped walnuts
½ cup raisins

Heat oven to 350°. Spray a 12-cup muffin pan with cooking spray. In a medium bowl, beat egg. Alternate adding oil and honey, using the same spoon (honey will slide off easily), and continue to blend. Add buttermilk and blend thoroughly.

In a separate bowl combine bran, flour, baking powder, baking soda and salt. Gradually add the dry mixture to the wet mixture. Blend only until moistened. Add walnuts and raisins and mix only until blended. Do not over blend.

Equally divide batter among 12 muffin cups and bake for 13 to 20 minutes, until golden brown, but moist. A toothpick should come out clean.

VARIATIONS ON A THEME

Bran: Wheat bran is suggested, but oat bran works well for a milder taste and its health benefits. I've even used uncooked hot cereal such as Cream of Wheat or Cream of Rice.

Flour: Instead of 1¼ cups of whole-wheat flour, substitute ½ cup white flour and ¾ cup whole-wheat flour to create a lighter muffin. Feel free to experiment with other flours and proportions.

Oil: Many types of oil can be used, e.g. canola or vegetable. Avoid using strongly flavored oils such as extra virgin olive oil.

Raisins: Any type of raisin can be used. So can any dried fruit cut into raisin-sized chunks, such as apricots, prunes, pears, papaya, figs, etc.

Walnuts: Using a variety of nuts works well. My favorites are: pecans, lightly toasted almond slivers, and macadamia nuts, (roasted without salt). Peanuts are too bitter to be used.

Low-Fat Buttermilk: You can substitute whole milk, skim milk or canned milk. You can also substitute yogurt. If you use flavored yogurt, be sure that the type of fruit you are using is compatible with the yogurt's flavor.

Egg: You can use egg substitute for less cholesterol, but it may cause the muffins to stick to the pan.

ADDITIONS TO YOUR BRAN MUFFIN

Fresh fruits give a variety of textures to your muffins. For example: mashed banana; peeled and chopped apple or peach. Make sure fruit is cut very small, mashed or grated. Sweet spices also work well. Try cinnamon; nutmeg and allspice; or cardamom.

APPLE NUT BRAN MUFFINS

Add 1 cup peeled, grated apples with the raisins and nuts.

BANANA NUT BRAN MUFFINS

Mix 1 mashed banana with wet ingredients and omit raisins.

APRICOT PEACH BRAN MUFFINS

Add 1 cup peeled, chopped peaches, and replace raisins with chopped dried apricots.

CORN MUFFINS

Fresh or frozen corn gives this traditional muffin a wonderful texture. Eaten with eggs, they're a great change from toast or biscuits.

nonstick cooking spray
1/2 cup all-purpose flour
1 1/2 cups cornmeal
2 tsp. baking powder
1/2 tsp. baking soda
1/4 tsp. salt

2 tbs. sugar
2 eggs
1/2 cup vegetable oil
1 1/2 cups buttermilk
1 cup corn, fresh or frozen

Heat oven to 350°. Spray a 12-cup muffin pan with cooking spray. Combine flour, cornmeal, baking powder, baking soda, salt and sugar, and set aside.

In another bowl, beat eggs and add oil, then buttermilk. Combine the two mixtures, just until blended, then gently fold in corn just until blended.

Divide batter evenly among 12 muffin cups. Bake for 13 to 20 minutes. A toothpick should come out clean.

NEW YORK CORN MUFFINS

For a sweeter version of traditional muffins, increase sugar to one cup and add 1 tsp. vanilla extract.

CARROT WHEAT GERM MUFFINS

Toasted wheat germ adds to the flavor and texture of these muffins. The taste is very much like carrot cake.

nonstick cooking spray
1½ cups flour
½ cup toasted wheat germ
2 tsp. baking powder
¼ tsp. salt
1 tsp. cinnamon
½ tsp. nutmeg
¼ tsp. allspice

1 cup sugar
½ cup (1 stick) margarine
1 egg
½ cup milk
1 cup firmly packed grated carrots
½ cup chopped walnuts

Heat oven to 350°. Spray a 12-cup muffin pan with cooking spray. In a bowl combine flour, wheat germ, baking powder, salt, cinnamon, nutmeg and allspice. In a second bowl, with an electric mixer, cream sugar and margarine until well blended. In a third bowl, beat egg and add milk.

Alternately add flour mixture and egg mixture to the creamed margarine/sugar mixture just until blended. Add carrots and walnuts and mix just until blended.

Divide evenly among 12 muffin cups and bake for 17 to 25 minutes. Muffins are done when a toothpick comes out clean.

CARROT WHEAT GERM DATE MUFFINS

Add 1 cup chopped dates with the carrots and walnuts.

ORANGE PINEAPPLE MUFFINS

The combination of orange and pineapple is tart and sweet. The dried fruit gives a chewy texture.

nonstick cooking spray
1 cup dried pineapple
1¹/₂ cups all-purpose flour
1 cup sugar
1 tsp. baking powder
¹/₂ tsp. baking soda
¹/₄ tsp. salt
1 egg

¹/₄ cup (¹/₂ stick) melted
  margarine
1 tsp. orange extract
1 eight oz. can crushed
  pineapple
¹/₂ cup orange juice
2 tsp. grated orange peel (zest)

Heat oven to 350°. Spray a 12-cup muffin pan with cooking spray. Cut dried pineapple into raisin-sized chunks.

Mix flour, sugar, baking powder, baking soda and salt. Set aside. In a large bowl, beat egg and add margarine, orange extract, crushed pineapple, orange juice and zest. Add dry ingredients gradually into wet ingredients and blend thoroughly. Mix in dried pineapple, only until blended.

Divide batter evenly among 12 muffin cups. Bake for 13 to 20 minutes. Top should be lightly browned. If a toothpick does not come out clean, return to the oven another three minutes and recheck.

CRANBERRY ORANGE BRAN MUFFINS ♥

This is a low-fat, high-fiber recipe. The addition of bran makes this an even healthier recipe. Great for the holidays or any time. The tart taste of cranberries works well with sweet taste of the muffin. If a sweeter berry is desired, use the variation below.

nonstick cooking spray
1½ cups all-purpose flour
1 cup sugar
3 tsp. baking powder
¼ tsp. baking soda
1 cup bran
¾ cup chopped walnuts or
    pecans

1 egg
1 cup 2% reduced fat milk
2 tbs. vegetable oil
½ cup applesauce
2 tsp. grated orange zest
1½ cups whole cranberries

Heat oven to 350°. Spray a 12-cup muffin pan with cooking spray. Combine flour, sugar, baking powder, banking soda and bran and set aside. In a separate bowl beat egg and mix with milk, oil, applesauce, and zest until thoroughly blended. Pour wet ingredients into dry mixture and blend just until smooth. Add nuts and stir until evenly distributed. Gently stir in cranberries.

Divide batter evenly among 12 muffin cups. Bake for 13 to 20 minutes. Make sure toothpick comes out clean (remember not to count moisture from cranberries).

SWEETER CRANBERRY ORANGE BRAN MUFFINS

Replace fresh cranberries with dried cranberries (plain or flavored craisins).

BANANAS AND CREAM MUFFINS

Each muffin is like a miniature loaf of moist banana bread.

nonstick cooking spray
$\frac{1}{2}$ cup (1 stick) margarine
1 cup sugar
2 cups sifted all-purpose flour
2 tsp. baking powder
$\frac{1}{2}$ tsp. baking soda
$\frac{1}{4}$ tsp. salt

2 very ripe bananas, mashed
2 eggs
3 tbs. sour cream
1 tsp. vanilla extract
$\frac{1}{2}$ cup chopped walnuts or
  pecans

Heat oven to 350°. Spray a 12-cup muffin pan with cooking spray. With an electric mixer, cream margarine and sugar and set aside. In a separate bowl mix flour, baking powder, baking soda and salt until completely blended.

In a third bowl, beat eggs and mix with bananas, sour cream and vanilla, making sure all ingredients are well blended.

Alternately add dry mixture and wet mixture to margarine/sugar mixture. Mix in nuts only until blended.

Divide batter evenly among 12 muffin cups. Bake for 12 to 20 minutes, until toothpick comes out clean.

LOWER FAT BANANAS AND CREAM MUFFINS

Use egg substitute instead of eggs; use fat-free sour cream instead of sour cream; use light margarine instead of margarine; and eliminate nuts.

PLUM OAT MUFFINS

The batter is thick and will yield 15 muffins. If you don't have an extra muffin pan, refrigerate the remaining batter, covered, until ready to use. When baking less than a full batch, fill the empty muffin cups halfway with water to prevent smoking.

nonstick cooking spray

2–3 large fresh plums (any type but greengage), about 1/2–3/4 lb.

2 cups all-purpose flour

1 cup quick oats

1/2 cup brown sugar, firmly packed

1/2 cup granulated sugar

2 tsp. baking powder

1/2 tsp. baking soda

1 tsp. ground coriander

1/4 tsp. salt

1 egg

1 tsp. vanilla extract

1/3 cup vegetable oil

1 cup milk

Heat oven to 350°. Spray a 12-cup muffin pan with cooking spray. Chop plums into small chunks and set aside.

In a separate bowl combine flour, oats, brown sugar, granulated sugar, baking powder, baking soda, coriander and salt until well blended, making sure that all the lumps in the sugar are gone. Set aside.

In another bowl, beat egg. Add vanilla, oil and milk. Add wet mixture to dry mixture until well blended. Batter will be thick. Gently fold in plums. Equally divide batter among the 12 muffin cups. Cover and refrigerate any remaining batter. Bake for 13 to 20 minutes, just until the toothpick comes out clean.

OFF-SEASON PLUM OAT MUFFINS

If plums are out of season, or as an alternative, replace plums with 2 cups of dried plums or prunes.

APRICOT OATMEAL MUFFINS

Apricot lovers beware! Every bite is loaded with apricots.

nonstick cooking spray
1 1/2 cups whole-wheat flour
2 1/2 tsp. baking powder
1/2 tsp. baking soda
1/8 tsp. salt
1 cup quick-cooking oatmeal, uncooked
1/4 cup sugar

1/2 cup brown sugar, firmly packed
1/2 cup (1 stick) margarine
1 egg
1 1/4 cup buttermilk
3 cup dried apricots (about 1 lb.), chopped into raisin-sized chunks

Heat oven to 375°. Spray a 12-cup muffin pan with cooking spray. Combine flour, baking powder, baking soda, salt, and oatmeal. Set aside.

In a separate large bowl, using an electric mixer, cream both sugars and the margarine until smooth. In a third, small bowl, lightly beat egg and add buttermilk.

Alternate adding dry and wet ingredients to margarine/sugar mixture, beginning with dry, until thoroughly blended

Divide evenly among muffin cups and bake for 22-30 minutes, until firm but moist. Toothpick should come out clean. Muffins may have a slight crust.

PEACH OAT MUFFINS
Replace dried apricots with dried peaches.

PEANUT BUTTER MUFFINS

These muffins are wonderful just the way they are, and of course they are perfect with jelly.

nonstick cooking spray
1½ cups all-purpose flour
¼ tsp. salt
2½ tsp. baking powder

1 cup sugar
⅔ cup crunchy peanut butter
1 egg, lightly beaten
1 cup 2% reduced fat milk

Heat oven to 350°. Spray a 12-cup muffin pan with cooking spray. Combine flour, salt and baking powder. Set aside.

In another bowl, blend sugar into peanut butter. Mixture will be crumbly. Add beaten egg and blend until smooth. Gradually add milk and blend well.

Gently stir dry mixture into wet mixture only until evenly blended. Divide batter evenly among 12 muffin cups. Bake for 13 to 20 minutes. The top of the muffins should be lightly browned and a toothpick should come out clean.

PEANUT BUTTER CHOCOLATE CHIP MUFFINS

Gently fold ½ cup mini chocolate chips to batter after combing the wet and dry ingredients. Bake as directed.

CASHEW BUTTER MUFFINS

Replace peanut butter with cashew butter and fold in ½ cup chopped, roasted, unsalted cashews to the finished batter.

ALMOND BUTTER MUFFINS

Replace peanut butter with almond butter and fold in ½ cup chopped, roasted, peeled, unsalted almonds to the finished batter.

CHOCOLATE DATE NUT MUFFINS

The mild chocolate flavor of these muffins is complemented by the mellow flavor of the dates.

nonstick cooking spray
1/4 cup (1/2 stick) margarine
1/4 cup chocolate chips
1/2 cup plain, fat-free yogurt
1/2 cup 2% reduced fat milk
1 egg, beaten
2 cups all-purpose flour
1 cup sugar
1 tsp. baking powder

1/2 tsp. baking soda
1/4 tsp. salt
3 tbs. cocoa powder
1/2 cup chopped walnuts
1 cup chopped dates

Heat oven to 350°. Spray a 12-cup muffin pan with cooking spray. In a small saucepan, melt margarine on low heat. Mix in chocolate chips and stir until mixture is melted and ingredients are completely incorporated. Remove from heat. Add yogurt, then milk, stirring after each until smooth. Gradually blend egg into mixture.

In a separate bowl, combine flour, sugar, baking powder, baking soda, salt and cocoa. Add chocolate mixture, blending gently until just combined. Carefully fold in walnuts and dates.

Divide batter evenly among 12 muffin cups and bake 17 to 25 minutes, or until toothpick comes out clean. Do not over-bake.

MARBLE CHIP MUFFINS

These muffins are like miniature marble cakes. Instead of chocolate icing, I used chocolate chips for an extra chocolate accent.

nonstick cooking spray
$\frac{1}{2}$ cup (1 stick) plus 3 tbs.
   margarine
$\frac{3}{4}$ cup plus 2 tsp. sugar
$1\frac{1}{2}$ cups all-purpose flour
2 tsp. baking powder
$\frac{1}{2}$ tsp. baking soda
$\frac{1}{4}$ tsp. salt

1 egg
$\frac{1}{2}$ cup plus 3 tbs. evaporated
   milk
1 tsp. vanilla extract
$\frac{1}{2}$ cup chopped walnuts
1 cup chocolate chips
$\frac{1}{3}$ cup cocoa powder

Heat oven to 350°. Spray a 12-cup muffin pan with cooking spray. Blend $\frac{1}{2}$ cup of the margarine and sugar until smooth. Set aside. In a sifter or strainer, combine flour, baking powder, baking soda and salt. Sift and set aside. In a third bowl, lightly beat egg. Add milk and vanilla. Alternate adding flour mixture and egg mixture to margarine/sugar mixture. Add nuts and chocolate chips and combine, only until blended.

In a saucepan over low heat, combine remaining 3 tbs. margarine and 3 tbs. milk, cocoa and remaining 2 tsp. sugar. Remove ⅓ of the batter and completely blend with cocoa mixture.

Divide remaining ⅔ of the batter (not cocoa batter) among 12 muffin cups. Spoon even amounts of cocoa batter onto each of the 12 cups. Use a knife or bamboo skewer to swirl batter to marbleize, taking care not to completely blend. Bake for 13 to 20 minutes, until a toothpick comes out clean.

MARBLE MARBLE CHIP MUFFINS

Substitute ½ cup white chocolate chips for ½ cup chocolate chips.

POPPY SEED MUFFINS

The crunchy nuttiness of poppy seeds and walnuts combine with the tanginess of orange peel and the fruitiness of golden raisins.

nonstick cooking spray
2 tbs. poppy seeds
1/4 cup (1/2 stick) margarine, softened
3/4 cup sugar
2 tsp. orange zest
2 eggs
1/2 tsp. vanilla extract

1/8 tsp. almond extract
2 cups all-purpose flour
2 1/2 tsp. baking powder
1/4 tsp. salt
1/4 tsp. ground nutmeg
1 cup milk
1 cup golden raisins
1/2 cup chopped walnuts

Heat oven to 400°. Spray a 12-cup muffin pan with cooking spray. Put poppy seeds on a cookie sheet and bake for 5 minutes, until toasted, then put in a dish to cool. Reduce oven temperature to 350°.

With an electric mixer, cream sugar and margarine. Add orange zest. Add eggs one at a time, beating after each addition. Add vanilla and almond extracts to mixture. In a separate bowl combine flour, baking powder, salt and nutmeg.

By hand, gently alternate adding flour mixture and milk to margarine mixture. Blend just until all ingredients are incorporated. Fold in raisins, nuts and poppy seeds.

Divide evenly among 12 muffin cups. Bake for 18 to 25 minutes. The muffins should not be brown on top. The toothpick should come out clean.

RAISIN SPICE MUFFINS

This recipe has a flavor that is a cross between gingerbread and spice cake. If you prefer a stronger ginger flavor, increase the ginger to 1½ or 2 tsp.

nonstick cooking spray
2 eggs
½ cup honey
½ cup molasses
6 tbs. vegetable oil
½ cup plain yogurt
2 tsp. orange (or lemon) zest
2 cups whole-wheat flour

2 tsp. baking powder
½ tsp. baking soda
2 tsp. cinnamon
1 tsp. ginger
¼ tsp. salt
¼ tsp. ground cloves
1 cup raisins (or dried
    currants)

Heat the oven to 350°. Spray a 12-cup muffin pan with cooking spray. In a large bowl, lightly beat eggs. Add honey, molasses, oil, yogurt and zest and combine well.

In a separate bowl combine flour, baking powder, baking soda, cinnamon, ginger, salt and cloves. Add to wet ingredients and thoroughly blend. Carefully fold in raisins.

Divide batter evenly among 12 muffin cups. Bake for 13 to 20 minutes, until muffins are firm and toothpick comes out clean.

RICH AND MOIST
CURRANT BRAN MUFFINS ♥

This is a low-fat, high-fiber recipe. These muffins are light, porous, and are very low in fat.

nonstick cooking spray
1/2 cup egg substitute
1 cup fat-free sour cream
1/2 cup 2% or skim milk
3/4 cup bran
1/4 cup vegetable oil
1 cup all-purpose flour

1/2 cup brown sugar, packed
1 tsp. baking powder
1/2 tsp. baking soda
1/4 tsp. salt
1/2 cup granulated sugar
3/4 cup dried currants

Heat oven to 350°. Spray a 12-cup muffin pan with cooking spray. In a medium bowl, combine egg substitute, sour cream and milk. Stir in bran. Let mixture stand for 5 minutes, or until all

liquid is absorbed, then add oil.

In a separate large bowl, combine flour, brown sugar, baking powder, baking soda, salt and granulated sugar, making sure to remove all lumps.

Make a well in the center of the dry ingredients and add the egg mixture all at once. Stir only until mixture is moistened, then fold in the currants. Do not over mix.

Divide evenly among the 12 muffin cups and bake 13 to 18 minutes, until a toothpick comes out clean.

RICHER AND MOISTER CURRANT BRAN MUFFINS

Make the following substitutions: 2 eggs for egg substitute; regular sour cream for fat-free sour cream; whole milk for skim milk.

BLUEBERRY MUFFINS

These are the best blueberry muffins I've tasted.

nonstick cooking spray
2 cups all-purpose flour
2 tsp. baking powder
1/4 tsp. salt
1/2 cup (1 stick) margarine
3/4 cup sugar
1 egg
1 cup milk
1/2 tsp. vanilla extract
1 1/2 cups fresh blueberries*

Heat oven to 350°. Spray a 12-cup muffin pan with cooking spray. Mix together flour, baking powder and salt. Set aside.

With an electric mixer, cream margarine and sugar until light and fluffy. Set aside. In a separate bowl, lightly beat egg and combine with milk and vanilla.

Alternately add dry mixture and wet mixture into the creamed margarine/sugar mixture, just until blended. Gently fold in the blueberries. Try to avoid breaking them. They are fragile.

Divide the batter evenly among the 12 cups. Bake for 18 to 25 minutes. A toothpick should come out clean.

*Frozen blueberries can be substituted, but fresh are easier to work with.

RASPBERRY MUFFINS

Substitute raspberries for blueberries, fresh or frozen.

APPLE PUMPKIN BRAN MUFFINS

These muffins have a moist and heavy texture. Only ¼ cup of milk is needed because of the moisture from the pumpkin. If you like pumpkin bread you'll love this recipe.

nonstick cooking spray
1 cup bran
¼ cup milk
2 eggs
¾ cup pumpkin puree
1 cup sugar
4 tbs. margarine
1¼ cups all-purpose flour

1½ tsp. baking powder
½ tsp. baking soda
2½ tsp. pumpkin pie spice
¼ tsp. salt
1 cup chopped walnuts
1 medium apple, cored,
  peeled and finely chopped
  (about 1 cup)

Heat oven to 325°. Spray a 12-cup muffin pan with cooking spray. In a medium bowl, combine bran, milk and eggs. Let stand for 5 minutes, then combine with pumpkin. Set aside.

In a second large bowl, with an electric mixer, cream sugar and margarine till well blended. Add bran mixture and combine well.

In a third bowl, thoroughly blend flour, baking powder, baking soda, pumpkin pie spice and salt. Gradually add the flour mixture to the bran mixture and blend till smooth. Add nuts and apple.

Divide evenly among 12 muffin cups and bake 22 to 30 minutes. Muffins are done when a toothpick comes out clean.

FRUIT AND NUT MUFFINS ♥

This is a low-fat, high-fiber recipe. These muffins are almost a meal by themselves. They include the four basic food groups.

nonstick cooking spray
1/2 cup whole-wheat flour
1/2 cup all-purpose flour
1/2 cup uncooked oatmeal
1/2 cup bran
1/4 tsp. salt
1/2 tsp. cinnamon
2 tsp. baking powder
1/4 tsp. baking soda
1/4 tsp. nutmeg

3/4 cup sugar
5 tbs. margarine
1 egg, beaten
1/4 cup applesauce
1 medium-sized ripe banana, mashed
1/2 cup plain yogurt
3/4 cup sunflower seeds, roasted and salted
1 cup chopped dried apricots

Heat oven to 350°. Spray a 12-cup muffin pan with cooking spray. Combine both flours, oatmeal, bran, salt, cinnamon, baking powder, baking soda and nutmeg. Set aside.

In a separate bowl, with an electric mixer, cream sugar and margarine. Mixture will be crumbly. Add egg, applesauce, banana and yogurt.

Combine wet and dry ingredients by hand, just until moistened. Add sunflower seeds and apricots, just until combined.

Divide batter evenly among 12 muffin cups. Bake for 17 to 25 minutes, until firm and a toothpick comes out clean.

SWEET POTATO MUFFINS

Think sweet potato pie in a muffin. Make sure to only use baked sweet potatoes to avoid excess water from boiling, and incompatible flavors from prepared sweet potatoes.

cooking spray
4 tbs. margarine
1 cup sugar
1 egg, beaten slightly
2 small baked sweet potatoes,
   cooled to room temperature

1 cup flour
2 tsp. baking powder
$\frac{1}{2}$ tsp. baking soda
$\frac{1}{2}$ tsp. salt
1 tsp. pumpkin pie spice
$\frac{1}{2}$ cup chopped walnuts

Heat oven to 350°. Spray a 12 cup muffin tin with cooking spray. Combine margarine and sugar. It will be a sandy consistency. Add egg.

Cut sweet potatoes in half and scoop out insides. Mash with fork until smooth. Add sweet potato to egg mixture.

In a separate bowl, combine flour, baking powder, baking soda, salt, and pumpkin pie spice.

Combine wet mixture into dry mixture only until blended. Add walnuts. Evenly divide batter among 12 muffin cups. Bake for 15 to 20 minutes, until a toothpick comes out clean.

CHERRY VANILLA MUFFINS

Vanilla muffins combine with cherry filling to create an unbeatable combination.

nonstick cooking spray
1 egg
1 cup milk or buttermilk
1 tsp. vanilla extract
4 tbs. margarine, melted
2 cups all-purpose flour
1 cup sugar
2$\frac{1}{2}$ tsp. baking powder
$\frac{1}{2}$ tsp. baking soda
$\frac{1}{4}$ tsp. salt
1 cup cherry pie filling

Heat oven to 350°. Spray a 12-cup muffin pan with cooking spray. In a small bowl, lightly beat egg. Add milk, vanilla and margarine. The margarine will float on the egg mixture. Set aside.

In a separate large bowl, combine flour, sugar, baking powder, baking soda and salt. Gradually add the wet mixture.

Measure out the cherry pie filling, taking care to pack in as many cherries and as little liquid as possible. Gently blend the cherry filling into the batter so as not to break the cherries.

Divide batter evenly among 12 muffin cups. Bake for 12 to 20 minutes. They will be very moist, but make sure a toothpick comes out clean.

MAPLE WALNUT MUFFINS

My inspiration was maple walnut ice cream. The flavor of maple is mild. For a stronger flavor, break open these muffins and serve them with butter and maple syrup

3/4 cup chopped walnuts, divided
nonstick cooking spray
2 cups all-purpose flour
2 tsp. baking powder
1/4 tsp. salt
1/2 cup margarine
3/4 cup sugar
1 egg
1 cup milk
2 tsp. maple extract

Heat oven to 400°. Place the chopped walnuts on a cookie sheet and bake for 4 minutes. Cool completely. Reduce oven to 350°. Spray a 12-cup muffin pan with cooking spray.

Mix together flour, baking powder and salt. Set aside. With an electric mixer, cream margarine and sugar until light and fluffy. Set aside. In a separate bowl, beat egg. Add milk and maple extract. Alternate adding dry and wet mixtures, by hand, into the creamed margarine/sugar mixture just until blended. Fold in ½ cup of the walnuts.

Divide the batter evenly among the 12 cups. Sprinkle the muffins with the remaining ¼ cup walnuts. Bake for 18 to 23 minutes. A toothpick should come out clean.

MAPLE PECAN MUFFINS

Substitute pecans for walnuts.

COCONUT CHOCOLATE CHIP MUFFINS

This muffin is reminiscent of a candy bar, with chocolate, nuts and coconut, but is flexible to allow for creativity.

nonstick cooking spray
³/₄ cup sweetened coconut
   flakes, firmly packed
2 cups all-purpose flour
2 tsp. baking powder
¹/₄ tsp. salt
¹/₂ cup (1 stick) margarine

¹/₂ cup granulated sugar
¹/₂ cup brown sugar, packed
1 egg
1 cup milk
1 tsp. vanilla extract
¹/₂ cup chocolate chips
¹/₂ cup chopped walnuts

Heat the oven to 350°. Spray a 12-cup muffin pan with cooking spray. Spread ¹/₂ cup of the coconut on a cookie sheet and bake for 7 to 10 minutes, stirring frequently to prevent burning (coconut should be light brown). Mix together flour, baking powder and salt. Set aside. With an electric mixer, cream margarine and both sugars until light and fluffy. Set aside. In a third bowl, beat egg. Add milk and vanilla extract. Alternate adding dry and wet mixtures into the creamed margarine/sugar mixture just until blended. Fold in toasted coconut, chocolate chips and walnuts. Divide batter evenly among the 12 cups. Sprinkle muffins with remaining 1/4 cup coconut. Bake for 17 to 25 minutes. Cool completely. Twist while removing muffins, to avoid sticking.

COCONUT BUTTERSCOTCH CHIP MUFFINS

Substitute butterscotch chips for chocolate chips; 1 tsp. rum extract for vanilla extract; and pecans for walnuts.

COCONUT WHITE CHOCOLATE CHIP MACADAMIA MUFFINS

Use white chocolate chips for chocolate chips; macadamia nuts for walnuts.

HAM AND CHEESE MUFFINS

nonstick cooking spray
2 cups all-purpose flour
2 1/2 tsp. baking powder
1/4 tsp. ground black pepper
1/2 tsp. salt
1 tsp. dried dill
1 egg beaten
1 1/2 cups milk
1/2 cup ham, finely shredded
1 cup American or cheddar cheese, finely grated

Heat oven to 350°. Spray a 12-cup muffin pan with cooking spray. Combine flour, baking powder, pepper, salt and dill together and set aside.

In a separate bowl, combine egg and milk. Combine with dry mixture just until blended. Add ham and cheese.

Divide batter evenly among 12 cups. Bake for 15 to 20 minutes.

HAM AND CHEESE ON RYE MUFFINS

Substitute caraway seeds for dill weed.

CHILI CHEESE MUFFINS

Picture a steaming bowl of chili sprinkled with cheese and served with fresh baked bread, but combined in one easy-to-eat muffin.

nonstick cooking spray
1 tsp. fresh garlic, minced
½ lb. lean ground beef
1 tsp. vegetable oil
¼ tsp. freshly ground black
    pepper
2 tsp. chili powder
2 tsp. cumin
2 cups all-purpose flour

2½ tsp. baking powder
½ tsp. garlic powder
½ tsp. salt
1 egg
1¼ cups milk
1½ cups grated American
    cheese
¼ cup (½ stick) margarine,
    melted

Heat oven to 350°. Place minced garlic and beef in a pan with oil. Sautee until completely cooked. Drain off all the fat and set aside to cool. When cool, sprinkle with pepper, chili powder and cumin. Combine and set aside.

In a separate bowl, combine flour, baking powder, garlic powder and salt. Set aside.

In another bowl, lightly beat egg and add milk and cheese.

Combine wet and dry mixtures. Add margarine, then cooled beef.

Divide batter evenly among 12 muffin cups. Bake for 15 to 20 minutes, then turn up the oven to 450° and bake 3 additional minutes, until the tops are golden brown.

CHEESY JALAPEÑO CORN MUFFINS

The sweet goodness of a traditional corn muffin laced with cheese and spiced with jalapeños make these muffins irresistible.

nonstick cooking spray
1 1/4 cups all-purpose flour
3/4 cup cornmeal
1/4 cup sugar
2 tsp. baking powder
1/2 tsp. salt
1 1/2 cups 2% reduced fat milk
1 egg
1 1/2 tbs. seeded, finely minced jalapeño pepper
3/4 cup shredded American or cheddar cheese

Heat oven to 350°. Spray a 12-cup muffin pan with cooking spray. Combine flour, cornmeal, sugar, baking powder and salt. Set aside.

Mix milk and egg together till well blended. Add wet mixture to dry mixture. Blend in peppers and cheese just until evenly distributed.

Divide batter evenly among 12 muffin cups. Bake for 20 to 25 minutes.

EXTRA SPICY JALAPEÑO CHEESE CORN MUFFINS

Add an extra $\frac{1}{2}$ to 1 tbs. of jalapeño pepper for a spicier muffin.

FETA HERB MUFFINS

Feta cheese blends perfectly with olives and oregano to give this muffin a decidedly Greek flavor.

nonstick cooking spray
2 cups all-purpose flour
2½ tsp. baking powder
½ tsp. baking soda
2 tsp. dried oregano
¼ tsp. freshly ground pepper
¼ tsp. salt
1 egg

¼ cup (½ stick) margarine, melted
1¼ cups milk
1 cup finely crumbled feta cheese
¼ cup finely chopped black Mediterranean olives, well drained (not canned)

Heat oven to 350°. Spray a 12-cup muffin pan with cooking spray. Combine flour, baking powder, baking soda, oregano, pepper and salt. Set aside.

In a large bowl, beat egg. Drizzle margarine gradually, blending all the while, until thoroughly incorporated. Gradually add milk to this mixture.

Gradually mix the dry ingredients into the wet mixture, just until blended. Add feta and olives.

Divide batter evenly among 12 muffin cups. Bake for 17 to 25 minutes, until a toothpick comes out clean.

MUSHROOM SWISS CHEESE MUFFINS

Mushrooms and Swiss cheese are a natural combination, reminiscent of an omelet.

cooking spray
8–10 medium-sized mush-
    rooms
2 cups flour
2 tsp.baking powder
1/2 tsp. baking soda
1 tsp. freshly ground pepper
1 tbs. dried parsley

1 tsp. salt
4 tbs. margarine, melted
1 egg, slightly beaten
1 cup 2% reduced fat milk
1/2 cup chopped walnuts
1 cup finely grated swiss
    cheese

Heat oven to 350°. Spray a 12-cup muffin tin with cooking spray. Clean mushrooms with a damp cloth (do not wash them, because they will absorb too much water).

Finely chop mushrooms and set aside. There should be about 1½ cups of minced mushrooms. In another bowl combine, flour, baking powder, baking soda, pepper, parsley and salt. Set aside.

In a separate bowl, slowly blend margarine into egg. Gradually combine milk with egg-margarine mixture Add in mushrooms, walnuts and cheese.

Combine wet ingredients with dry ingredients and mix only until blended. Evenly divide batter among 12 muffin cups. Bake for 20 to 25 minutes.

VARIATIONS

Substitute other types of mushrooms such as portobello, crimini, or others.

Substitute other types of cheese such as cheddar, parmesan, or others.

ONION POPPY SEED MUFFINS

The inspiration for these muffins was a savory cookie recipe from my childhood.

cooking spray
2 cups flour
2 tsp. baking powder
1 tbs. poppy seeds
1/2 tsp. fresh ground pepper
1/2 tsp. salt
1 egg, slightly beaten
1/2 cup vegetable oil
1 cup 2% reduced fat milk
1 cup finely minced onions

Heat oven to 350°. Spray a 12-cup muffin tin with cooking spray. Combine flour, baking powder, poppy seeds, pepper and salt.

In a separate bowl, combine beaten egg, vegetable oil and milk. Blend wet mixture into dry mixture just until blended. Add onions, being careful not to over-mix.

Evenly divide batter among 12 muffin cups. Bake for 20 to 25 minutes, or until a toothpick comes out clean.

STUFFED POTATO MUFFINS

These muffins are a perfect way to use leftover baked potatoes.

cooking spray
4 strips bacon
2 cup flour
2 tsp. baking powder
½ tsp. baking soda
1 tsp. salt
3 tbs. sour cream

4 tbs. margarine, melted
1 egg, slightly beaten
1 cup 2% reduced fat milk
1 medium baked potato, at
    room temperature
1 cup shredded cheddar
½ cup thinly sliced scallions

Heat oven to 350°. Spray a 12-cup muffin tin with cooking spray. Cook bacon until crispy; drain, and crumble into bits. Set aside. Combine flour, baking powder, baking soda, and salt. Set aside.

In a separate bowl, gradually add sour cream and then melted margarine into egg. Add milk into egg mixture.

Cut potato in half and scoop out the insides. Press out all the lumps and combine with egg-sour cream-milk mixture. Add cheddar and scallions.

Add wet mixture into dry mixture just until blended. Divide muffin batter evenly among 12 muffin cups. Bake for 20 to 25 minutes, until a toothpick comes out clean.

VARIATIONS

Substitute Bacon Bits for bacon. Add fresh or dry parsley, cilantro or other herbs.

Substitute other types of cheese for cheddar, such as American, Swiss, or muenster.

Delete scallions or substitute with onions.

BACON, EGG, AND CHEESE MUFFINS

The classic combination of bacon, egg, and cheese, make these a natural for breakfast.

cooking spray
8 strips bacon
2 cup all purpose flour
2 tsp. baking powder
3/4 tsp. salt
1 egg, slightly beaten
2 tbs. bacon fat

1 tbs. vegetable oil
1 cup 2% reduced fat milk
1/2 cup finely shredded cheddar cheese
1 egg, hard boiled and chopped as for egg salad

Heat oven to 350°. Spray a 12 cup muffin tin with cooking spray. Cook bacon until crispy, and drain well on a paper towel. Crumble bacon into small bits and set aside.

Combine flour, baking powder and salt until well blended. Combine egg and slowly blend in bacon fat and vegetable oil. Gradually add milk, cheese, bacon, and chopped egg. Combine wet and dry mixtures just until blended.

Evenly divide batter among 12 muffin cups. Bake for 20 to 25 minutes, or until a toothpick comes out clean.

VEGETARIAN BACON, EGG, AND CHEESE MUFFINS

Replace bacon with Bacon Bits, and bacon fat with vegetable oil.

HAM, EGG, AND CHEESE MUFFIN

Replace bacon with ham.

COTTAGE CHEESE DILL MUFFINS

This recipe is based on an aromatic bread recipe. The double dose of dill gives these muffins a unique flavor that contrasts well with cottage cheese.

cooking spray
2 cups flour
2 1/2 tsp. baking powder
1/2 tsp. baking soda
1 tsp. dried dill
2 tsp. dill seed

3/4 tsp. salt
1 egg, slightly beaten
1 cup 2% reduced fat milk
2 tbs. melted margarine
2 cup small curd cottage
   cheese

Preheat oven to 350°. Spray a 12 cup muffin tin with cooking spray. Combine flour, baking powder, baking soda, dried dill, dill seed and salt together.

In a separate bowl, combine egg, milk, melted margarine and cottage cheese. Combine wet mixture with dry mixture and mix only until blended.

Divide evenly among 12 muffin cups. Bake for 20 minutes, or just until a toothpick comes out clean

ZUCCHINI PARMESAN MUFFINS

Typical zucchini bread tastes much like carrot bread, but in this savory recipe, the shredded Zucchini adds color and moisture and is complemented by the onions, cheese and spices.

cooking spray
1 medium zucchini
(about 1/2 lb.)
2 1/4 cups all purpose flour
2 tsp. baking powder
1/2 tsp. baking soda
1 tsp. garlic powder

1/2 tsp. freshly ground pepper
1/2 cup grated parmesan and
romano cheeses
1/2 cup olive oil
1 egg, slightly beaten
1 cup 2% reduced fat milk
1/2 cup finely chopped onion

Heat oven to 350°. Spray a 12 cup muffin tin with cooking spray. Clean zucchini and remove ends. Finely grate zucchini and squeeze out all excess water. Firmly pack zucchini into a one cup measure.

Combine flour, baking powder, baking soda, garlic powder, pepper and cheese.

In a separate bowl, slowly mix olive oil into egg. Gradually add milk until well blended. Add onion and zucchini.

Gradually add wet mixture into dry mixture, mixing just until blended. Evenly divide batter among 12 muffin cups. Bake for 20 to 25 minutes, or until a toothpick comes out clean.

PIZZA MUFFINS

As they are baking you'll smell the pizza aroma emanating from your oven. If you want to be daring, add some of your favorite pizza toppings to the recipe.

nonstick cooking spray
1¼ cups milk
1 egg
¼ cup olive oil
2 cups all-purpose flour
2 tsp. baking powder
¼ tsp. salt
½ cup grated Parmesan cheese
¼ tsp. freshly ground pepper

½ tsp. garlic powder
2 tsp. dried oregano
½ tsp. dried dill
½ tsp, dried basil
¾ cup sun-dried tomatoes, finely chopped (if packed in oil, drain and pat with a paper towel)

Heat oven to 350°. Spray a 12-cup muffin pan with cooking spray. Beat milk into egg. Beat in oil and set aside.

In a second bowl, combine flour, baking powder, salt, Parmesan, pepper, garlic powder and herbs. Combine wet and dry ingredients just until blended. Stir in tomatoes just until evenly distributed throughout batter.

Divide batter evenly among 12 muffin cups. Bake for 20 to 25 minutes. The toothpick should come out dry and the muffins should be slightly brown. This is a heavy muffin.

PIZZA MUFFIN VARIATIONS

SAUSAGE PIZZA MUFFINS

Cook ½ lb. of ground sausage, crumble, drain, and remove excess oil. Cool and add to the batter with the tomatoes.

OLIVE PIZZA MUFFINS

Add ½ cup chopped green and/or black olives, thoroughly drained, with the tomatoes.

MUSHROOM PIZZA MUFFINS

Add ½ cup cooked, finely chopped mushrooms (well drained), with the tomatoes.

SUPREME PIZZA MUFFINS

Add any combination of the above ingredients, or any others. If multiple ingredients are used, reduce the portion of each by half.

INDEX